First World War
and Army of Occupation
War Diary
France, Belgium and Germany

58 DIVISION
174 Infantry Brigade
London Regiment
2/7 Battalion
27 January 1917 - 31 January 1918

WO95/3005/8

The Naval & Military Press Ltd
www.nmarchive.com
Published in association with The National Archives

Published by

The Naval & Military Press Ltd

Unit 10 Ridgewood Industrial Park,

Uckfield, East Sussex,

TN22 5QE England

Tel: +44 (0) 1825 749494

www.naval-military-press.com

www.nmarchive.com

This diary has been reprinted in facsimile from the original. Any imperfections are inevitably reproduced and the quality may fall short of modern type and cartographic standards.

© **Crown Copyright**
Images reproduced by permission of The National Archives, London, England, 2015.

Contents

Document type	Place/Title	Date From	Date To
Heading	WO95/3005/8		
Heading	58 Division 174 Bde 2/7 London Regt 1915 Aug-1916 Feb 1917 Jan-1918 Jan		
War Diary	Havre	27/01/1917	29/01/1917
War Diary	Auxi-Le-Chateau	29/01/1917	30/01/1917
War Diary	Vacquerie-Le-Boucq	30/01/1917	02/02/1917
War Diary	Vacquerie	03/02/1917	05/02/1917
War Diary	Vacquerie Le Boucq	05/02/1917	05/02/1917
War Diary	Beau Repairec	06/02/1917	08/02/1917
War Diary	Berles Bienvillers	09/02/1917	13/02/1917
War Diary	Point V 22 Halloy	13/02/1917	20/02/1917
War Diary	Trenches Berles	20/02/1917	24/02/1917
Map	Fifth Army		
Map	Bullecourt Defences		
War Diary	Bailleulmont	25/02/1917	04/03/1917
War Diary	Humbercamp	05/03/1917	06/03/1917
War Diary	Berles-Au-Bois	07/03/1917	17/03/1917
War Diary	Bailleulmont	19/03/1917	22/03/1917
War Diary	Humbercamp	23/03/1917	28/03/1917
War Diary	Laherliere	29/03/1917	29/03/1917
War Diary	Grouches	30/03/1917	01/04/1917
War Diary	Vacquerie	02/04/1917	02/04/1917
War Diary	Regnauville	04/04/1917	04/04/1917
War Diary	Mailly-Maillet	05/04/1917	16/04/1917
War Diary	Bihucourt	16/04/1917	24/04/1917
Heading	War Diary of 2/7th Bn Lon Regt. From 25/4/17 To 24/5/17 Vol 5		
War Diary	Bihucourt	25/04/1917	15/05/1917
War Diary	Mory	16/05/1917	18/05/1917
War Diary	Ecoust	19/05/1917	22/05/1917
War Diary	Bullecourt	22/05/1917	23/05/1917
War Diary	Mory	24/05/1917	24/05/1917
Heading	War Diary of 2/7th London Regt. From 25/5/17 To 30/6/17 Vol 6		
War Diary	Mory	25/05/1917	28/05/1917
War Diary	Ecoust	29/05/1917	29/05/1917
War Diary	Bullecourt	30/05/1917	09/06/1917
War Diary	In Line	10/06/1917	13/06/1917
War Diary	Camps Near Mory	14/06/1917	15/06/1917
War Diary	Near Mory	16/06/1917	16/06/1917
War Diary	St. Leger	17/06/1917	19/06/1917
War Diary	In The Line	20/06/1917	23/06/1917
War Diary	St Leger	23/06/1917	23/06/1917
War Diary	Courcelles	24/06/1917	30/06/1917
Heading	War Diary of 2/7th London Regt. 1/7/17 To 31/7/17 Vol 7		
War Diary	Courcelles	01/07/1917	05/07/1917
War Diary	Bancourt	06/07/1917	06/07/1917
War Diary	Equancourt	07/07/1917	10/07/1917
War Diary	In The Line	10/07/1917	20/07/1917

War Diary	Metz-En-Couture	21/07/1917	28/07/1917
War Diary	Bertincourt	29/07/1917	31/07/1917
Map	Map 'A'		
War Diary	Simencourt	01/08/1917	26/08/1917
War Diary	Browne Camp Poperinghe	27/08/1917	27/08/1917
War Diary	Canal Bank	28/08/1917	31/08/1917
Heading	War Diary of 2/7th Battn The London Regt. From 1/9/17 To 30/9/17 Vol 9		
War Diary	In The Line	01/09/1917	02/09/1917
War Diary	Canal Bank	03/09/1917	05/09/1917
War Diary	Reigersberg Camp	06/09/1917	11/09/1917
War Diary	D Ambre Camp	11/09/1917	17/09/1917
War Diary	Reigersburg Camp	18/09/1917	18/09/1917
War Diary	In Line	19/09/1917	22/09/1917
War Diary	Reigersberg	22/09/1917	23/09/1917
War Diary	Brake Camp	24/09/1917	30/09/1917
Map	Map		
Miscellaneous	Message Form		
Map	Map		
Miscellaneous	Message Form		
Map	Map		
Miscellaneous	Message Form		
Map	Map		
Miscellaneous	Message Form		
Miscellaneous	2/7th Battalion The London Regiment	24/09/1917	24/09/1917
Miscellaneous	Appendix I Report on Action Taken By B. Coy 2/7th Bn. London Regt.	24/09/1917	24/09/1917
Miscellaneous	Appendix II		
Heading	War Diary of 2/7th Batt The London Regt. From 1/10/17 To 31/10/17 Vol 10		
War Diary	Bonningues-Lez-Ardres	01/10/1917	20/10/1917
War Diary	Poperinghe	21/10/1917	24/10/1917
War Diary	Siege Camp	24/10/1917	26/10/1917
War Diary	In The Line	26/10/1917	28/10/1917
War Diary	Kempton Park	29/10/1917	29/10/1917
War Diary	Canal Bank	30/10/1917	31/10/1917
War Diary	Siege Camp	01/11/1917	06/11/1917
War Diary	Canal Bank	07/11/1917	10/11/1917
War Diary	Siege Camp	11/11/1917	17/11/1917
War Diary	Herzeele	18/11/1917	30/11/1917
War Diary	Selles	01/12/1917	07/12/1917
War Diary	Seninghem	08/12/1917	08/12/1917
War Diary	Elverdinghe	09/12/1917	09/12/1917
War Diary	Kempton Park	10/12/1917	08/01/1918
War Diary	Road Camp	09/01/1918	19/01/1918
War Diary	Proven	20/01/1918	20/01/1918
War Diary	Moreuil	21/01/1918	31/01/1918

WO 95/30058

58 DIVISION

174 BDE

2/7 LONDON REGT

1915 AUG – 1916 FEB
1917 JAN – 1918 JAN

ABSORBED BY 1/7 BN 1918 FEB

Army Form C. 2118.

WAR DIARY
or
INTELLIGENCE SUMMARY.
(Erase heading not required.)

Instructions regarding War Diaries and Intelligence Summaries are contained in F. S. Regs., Part II. and the Staff Manual respectively. Title pages will be prepared in manuscript.

Place	Date	Hour	Summary of Events and Information	Remarks and references to Appendices
HAVRE	27/1/17	4·0 a.m.	First Half-Battalion landed from S.S. MONA'S QUEEN. Strength: 19 Officers (including M.O. + Chaplain) 569 Other ranks	
		12·0 noon	Marched to No. 1 Rest Camp (North) Second Half-Battalion landed from S.S. HUNTSCRAFT - Strength 14 Officers 423 Other ranks (including S. of F. men) 64 Horses + mules	
		9·0 p.m.	Marched to No. 1 Rest Camp (North) Orders for entrainment received from CAMP COMMANDANT (Col. F.J. PARKER) Vehicles as per establishment.	£B.7
	28/1/17	7·0 a.m.	Battalion (less 12 Officers + 400 O.R.) left Camp for POINT 3 (GARE DES MARCHANDISES) to entrain.	
		11·15 a.m.	" " " travelled out of HAVRE	
		5 p.m.	A Coy. (6 Officers + 200 O.R.) left Camp to entrain at POINT 3	
		6 p.m.	D Coy. (6 Officers + 200 O.R.) " " "	
		9·20 p.m.	A Coy. (as above) travelled out of HAVRE.	
		11·0 p.m.	D " " - " - " -	
	29/1/17	4 p.m.	Battalion (less A + D Coys. as above) detrained at AUXI-LE-CHATEAU. Orders received from STAFF-CAPTAIN, 174 Bde, to occupy billets at VACQUERIE-LE-BOUCQ. March to VACQUERIE, + occupy billets.	£B.7
AUXI-LE-CHATEAU	30/1/17	2·30 a.m.	A Coy. (as above) detrained at AUXI-LE-CHATEAU, + marched to billets at VACQUERIE.	
		1·30 a.m.	D " " " " FRÉVENT - " - " -	

Army Form C. 2118.

WAR DIARY
or
~~INTELLIGENCE SUMMARY~~

(Erase heading not required.)

Instructions regarding War Diaries and Intelligence Summaries are contained in F. S. Regs., Part II. and the Staff Manual respectively. Title pages will be prepared in manuscript.

Place	Date	Hour	Summary of Events and Information	Remarks and references to Appendices
VACQUERIE-LE-BOUCQ	30/1/17		Parade during day for inspection of arms, ammunition, clothing, equipment etc etc	LB7.
	31/1/17	9.45am	Companies carried out concentration march on BOUBERS-SUR-CANCHÉ	LB7.
	1/2/17	9.45am	" " " " " " — SERICOURT	
			Recruits } trained independently	LB7.
			Lewis gunners }
			Intelligence Section }
	2/2/17	9.0am	Recruit & Specialist training. Bayonet fighting.	
		1.15pm	Orders received from 174 BDE for working party of 1 Coy. to proceed to PAS on 3/2/17.	LB7.

Charles V. Berkeley
Lt-Col
2/7th Battn The London Regt
2/2/17

WAR DIARY
or
INTELLIGENCE SUMMARY

Army Form C. 2118.

(Erase heading not required.)

Place	Date	Hour	Summary of Events and Information	Remarks and references to Appendices
VACQUERIE	3.2.17	12·10 p.m.	"D" Coy (less details) proceeded by motor transport to PAS. Strength:— 4 Officers, 2 to DR, 6 Transport men, 2 RAMC Water duty men, 2 Wagon limbered GS, 1 Field Kitchen, 1 Water-cart. Totals 212 / 4	
	4.2.17	10·20 am	Parade for Recruits, Specialists etc.	
		3·40 p.m.	Church Parade.	
		11·50 p.m.	Message received that BATTN. would move to POMMERA on 5/2/17; march orders to follow.	D.R.O.
	5.2.17	10·0 am	March orders received from 174 BDE.	D.R.O.
			BATTN. paraded ready to move off for change of station.	D.R.O.

WAR DIARY
or
INTELLIGENCE SUMMARY.

(Erase heading not required.)

Army Form C. 2118.

Instructions regarding War Diaries and Intelligence Summaries are contained in F.S. Regs., Part II. and the Staff Manual respectively. Title pages will be prepared in manuscript.

Place	Date	Hour	Summary of Events and Information	Remarks and references to Appendices
VACQUERIE LES BOVES	5.2.17	10.45	Battalion marched out of VACQUERIE. Route BONNIÈRES – BOSQUE MAISON – LUCHEUX – L'ESPERANCE – BEAUREPAIRE.	1857.
BEAUREPAIRE	6.2.17	5.15 pm	Battalion arrived in billets at BEAUREPAIRE. Parades for inspection, roll-call etc.	1857.
	7.2.17	9.30 AM	Battalion paraded for route march. Route HALLOY – PAS – MONDICOURT. Special ids practised independently.	
		11.0 pm	Orders received from 19th BDE to proceed by motor-lorry to trenches at 10 AM on the 8th.	
	8.2.17	1.0 AM	Battalion less D Company proceeded by lorry to cross roads, point V.22, reference S.H. 61 C HOOGE.	
		4.30 pm	Battalion arrived in trenches "debussed". D Company arrived at point V.22 strength. D Company marched in from PAS. Orders received from 137th BDE for Battalion to occupy trenches for instruction.	
BERLES BIENVILLERS	9.2.17	4.0 pm	Occupation of trenches completed.	
	10.2.17	2.0 pm	1/6th S. STAFFORDS relieved by 1/5th S. STAFFORDS. Period of instruction continued.	
	11.2.17		Period of instruction continued.	
	12.2.17		Period of instruction continued. 1/5 S. STAFFORDS relieved by 1/6th S. ST AFFORDS. Orders received from 137th BDE to everyday trenches at HALLOY by 110 AM 13th.	
	13.2.17	7.0 am 10.45 am 10 AM	Battalion marched out of trenches to HALLOY by two from point V.22, to point V.22.	

WAR DIARY
INTELLIGENCE SUMMARY

Army Form C. 2118.

Place	Date	Hour	Summary of Events and Information	Remarks and references to Appendices
Pont V22.	13.2.17	5:30 pm	Battalion proceeded by motor-bus to HALLOY	ADS.
HALLOY	13.2.17	7.30 pm	Battalion arrived at HALLOY and proceeded into billets.	ADS.
	14.2.17		Company parades for changing billets, cleaning up, inspection etc	
	15.2.17	9.30 am	"B" and "C" Companies paraded for battalion drill under the Regimental Sgt Major	
		2.30 pm		
		4.30 pm	Companies paraded at intervals for inspection by the Commanding Officer	ADS.
	16.2.17	9.30 am	Companies paraded under O.C. Companies for fitting of box respirators, gas drill etc	
		2.30 am	Battalion paraded under Regimental Sgt Major for battalion drill. The following specialists paraded separately :- Batt. & Company Signallers, Lewis gunners & Instructional Class.	ADS.
			Intelligence Section.	
	17.2.17	9.30 am	"B" Company was inspected by Brig. Gen. the Briggs	
			"A" "C" "D" paraded for gas drill, physical training etc. Orders received from 14th Bde for battalion to proceed to HUMBERCAMP prior to proceeding to trenches to relieve 1/5th W.YORKS.	ADS.
	18.2.17	9.30 am	Battalion parade for divine service	
		11.0 am	fitting of Box RESPIRATORS.	
		9.0 pm	"B" "C" "D" Companies paraded for gas test	ADS.
	19.2.17	9.30 am	Battalion paraded and marched to HUMBERCAMP to relieve 1/5th W YORKS. Route HALLOY-PAS-FAMCHEMBRE	
	20.2.17	7.30 am	Battalion arrived from 136th Bde to relieve 1/5th W YORKS in trenches on 20.2.17 ADS. HUMBERCAMP - LA CAUCHIE - BAILLEULMONT Battalion marched by platoons to trenches ROUTE. HUMBERCAMP.	ADS.

Army Form C. 2118.

WAR DIARY
or
INTELLIGENCE SUMMARY.
(Erase heading not required.)

Instructions regarding War Diaries and Intelligence Summaries are contained in F. S. Regs., Part II. and the Staff Manual respectively. Title pages will be prepared in manuscript.

Place	Date	Hour	Summary of Events and Information	Remarks and references to Appendices
TRENCHES BERLES	20.2.17	4.30 AM	"D" Company proceed to BAILLEUL MONT in reserve	
	21.2.17	11.30 AM	Relief reports complete.	
	22.2.17		Period in trenches continued	
		11.10 PM	Order received from 174TH Bde for battalion to be relieved by 2/15TH LONDON REGT.	
	23.1.17		to billets at BAILLEULMONT	
			Period in trenches continued. No casualties.	
	24.1.17	9.10 AM	Battalion relieved in trenches by 2/15TH Batt. LONDON REGT. and proceeded to BAILLEULMONT	
		11.0 AM	to billets.	

Charles W. Berkeley
Lt Col

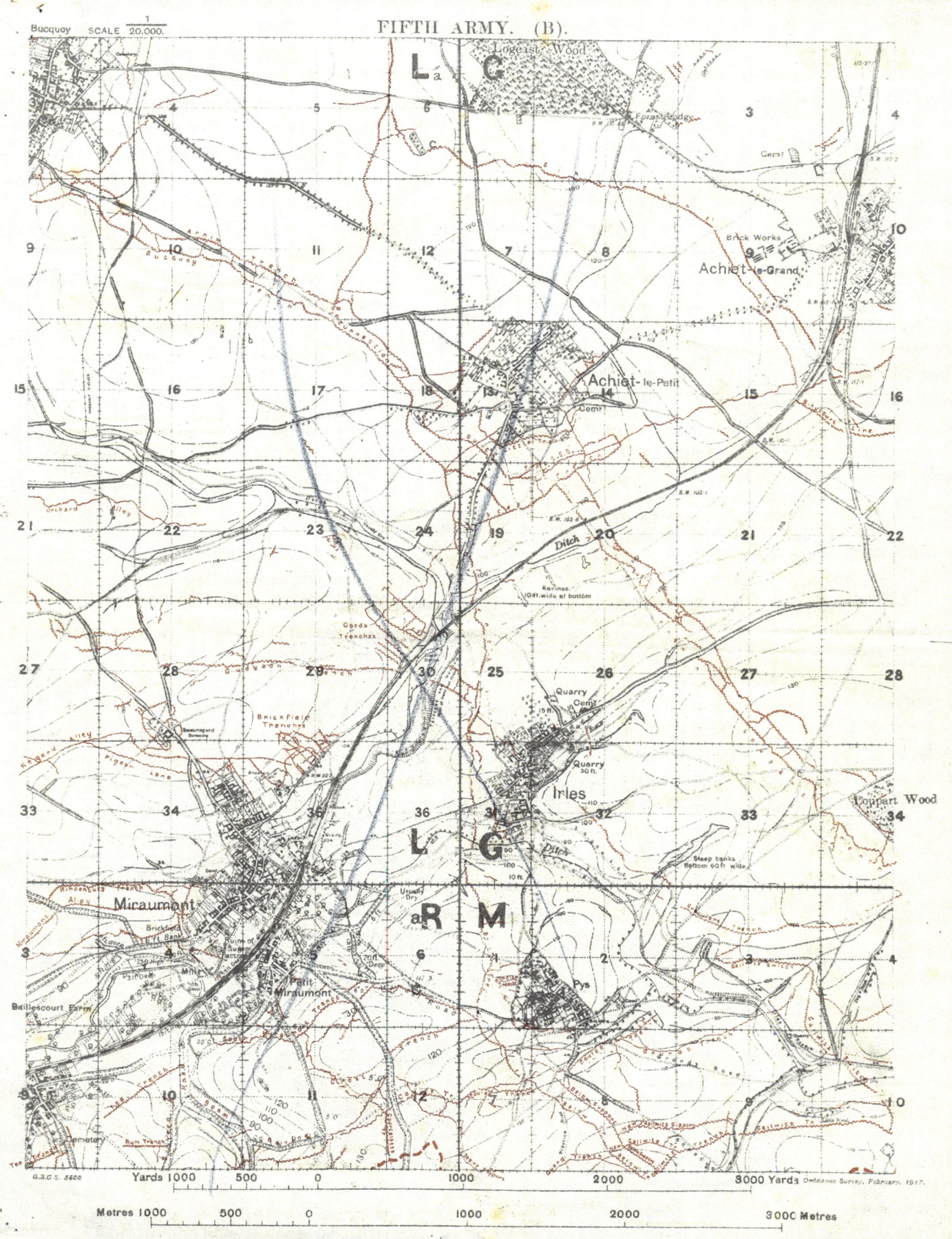

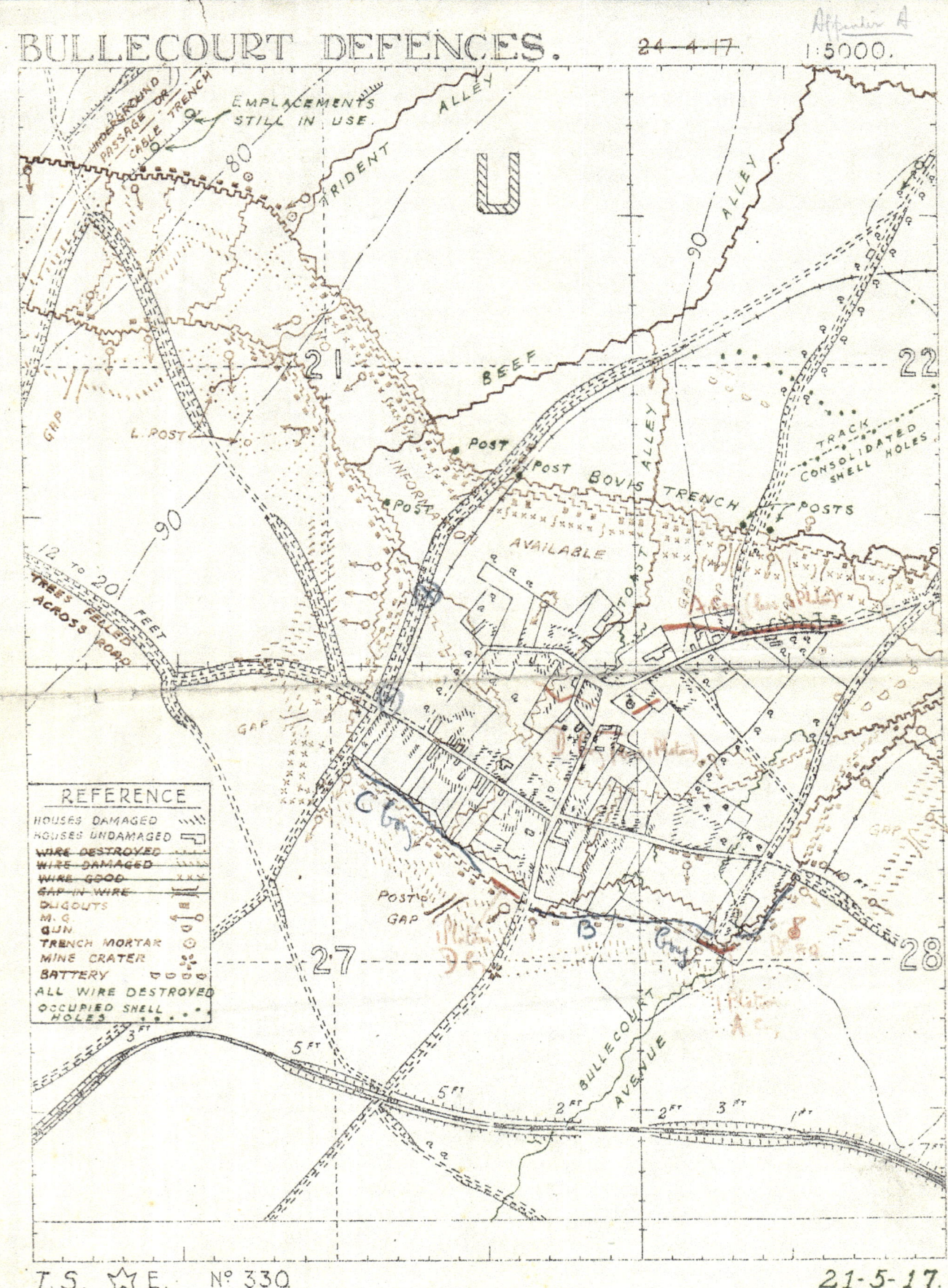

Army Form C. 2118.

2/7 London Regt

WAR DIARY
or
INTELLIGENCE SUMMARY.
(Erase heading not required.)

Instructions regarding War Diaries and Intelligence Summaries are contained in F. S. Regs., Part II. and the Staff Manual respectively. Title pages will be prepared in manuscript.

Place	Date	Hour	Summary of Events and Information	Remarks and references to Appendices
BAILLEULMONT	25.2.17		In billets in BAILLEULMONT.	
	26.2.17		}	
	27.2.17			
	28.2.17	12.15 p.m.	Battalion (less A.Coy) relieved 2/5 LONDON REGT. in trenches C1 sector in billets at BAILLEULMONT. A.Coy remained as Reserve Coy in billets at BAILLEULMONT.	A87
	4.3.17	1.15 p.m.	Battalion (less A.Coy) relieved by 2/5 LONDON REGT in trenches C1 Sector; marched to billets in HUMBERCAMP.	A87
		11.0 p.m.	A.Coy relieved by Coy of 2/5 LONDON; marched to billets at HUMBERCAMP.	
HUMBERCAMP			Orders received to relieve 1/6 SOUTH STAFFS in trenches @ Z2 sector.	A87
	5.3.17	9.30 p.m.	1/6 SOUTH STAFFS relieved in trenches Z2 sector.	
		11.0 p.m.	Orders received to withdraw three Coys from line on relief by 2/5 LONDON REGT, remaining Coy to hold a sector from N.23.c.80.55 to W.28.d.80.35 (MAP. SIC.SE.4. 1/10,000)	A87
	6.3.17		Relief in progress.	A87
	7.3.17	1.40 a.m.	Relief complete. Disposition of Companies. A.Coy. in line. B = Resting, to man DIVISIONAL LINE in billets BERLES. C = finding working parties etc. D = finding working parties etc. Standing to to reinforce	in billets BERLES A87
BERLES-AU-BOIS	9.3.17		Inter-company relief. Disposition - D.Coy in line. B finding working parties etc. C. Standing to to reinforce A. resting, to man DIVISIONAL LINE in BERLES	A87
	10.3.17		2/LT L. MILLER arrived as Reinforcement.	A87

LT. R.S. HUNT & 2/LT L. MILLER

Army Form C. 2118.

WAR DIARY
or
INTELLIGENCE SUMMARY.
(Erase heading not required.)

Instructions regarding War Diaries and Intelligence Summaries are contained in F.S. Regs., Part II. and the Staff Manual respectively. Title pages will be prepared in manuscript.

Place	Date	Hour	Summary of Events and Information	Remarks and references to Appendices
BERLES-AU-BOIS	11.3.17	4 p.m.	Orders received from 174 Bde. to relieve 1/4 Battn. entrenched with two Companies in place of one.	Bdr
	12.3.17		C Coy took over left half of frontage from D Coy.	
	13.3.17		B Coy relieved D Coy in Right Half of Bat. Frontage. A Coy — as Coy finding working parties. D — — At Rest	Bde
	17.3.17		Battalion relieved in BERLES sector (2 a.m.) by 2/8th LONDONS (P.O.R.). Enemy withdrew from MONCHY. Battalion moved to billets in BAILLEULMONT. Following officers and 1 OR. moved as reinforcements :— 2/Lts. C.W. KEAY, H. LAZENBY, R.K. LANGLEY, M. SHARP, P.W. HOOKER.	Bde Bde Bde
BAILLEULMONT	19.3.17		A Coy. proceeded to LA HERLIÈRE as working party. D — — LA CAUETTE	Bde
	20.3.17		Orders received to move to HUMBERCAMP on 22.3.17.	Bde
	22.3.17		Battalion moved to HUMBERCAMP. A & D Coys (less 1 Platoon of A Coy) rejoined from working parties.	Bde
HUMBERCAMP	23.3.17		Orders received to relieve 2/4th LONDON REGT. at BOISLEUX-AU-MONT on 25.3.17.	Bde
	24.3.17		Message received from 174 Bde. INEADE cancelling orders to move.	Bde

Charles W. Berkeley Lt. Col.

Army Form C. 2118.

WAR DIARY
or
INTELLIGENCE SUMMARY.
(Erase heading not required.)

2/4 Bn London Regt 303171815...

Vol 4

Place	Date	Hour	Summary of Events and Information	Remarks and references to Appendices
HUMBERCAMP	26/3/17		Companys & Specialist Training. ABR.	
	26/3/17		Orders received to march to billets in LAHERLIERE on 28/3/17. ABR.	
	27/3/17			
	28/3/17		Batt (less C & D Coys) marched to billets in LAHERLIERE. C & D Coys " " " - BAVINCOURT. ABR	
LAHERLIERE	29/3/17	10.30 pm	Orders received from 174th Inf. Bde. to march to billets in GROUCHES. ABR.	
	29/3/17		March to GROUCHES. Route: LARBRET - DOUELENS Road - MONDICOURT - MOULIN FERME - LUCHEUX - LUCHEUX. ABR.	
GROUCHES	30/3/17		Pltn of A Coy reported from detachment at GOMBREMETZ. ABR.	
	31/3/17		Inspection of Bompanies by Divl Gas Officer.	
	31/3/17	4.30 pm	Orders received to march to billets in VACQUERIE-LE-BOUCQ. ABR.	
	1/4/17		March to VACQUERIE-LE-BOUCQ. Route - LUCHEUX - BOUQUEMAISON - MAISON LEBLOND - BONNIÈRES - FORTEL - VACQUERIE. ABR.	
VACQUERIE	2/4/17		March to REGNAUVILLE - HAUTEVILLE. Route: ROUGEFAY - BURE-AU-BOIS - HARAVESNES - OUDEUX - CHERIENNE - REGNAUVILLE. B Coy & Transport to HAUTEVILLE. ABR.	
REGNAUVILLE	4/4/17	3 a.m.	Orders received to march to QUOEUX - FONTAINE road, to proceed thence by motor bus to MAILLY-MAILLET. Battalion reached MAILLY-MAILLET by 11.0 p.m. 4/4/17. Transport proceeded independently to AMPLIER. ABR.	

1577 Wt. W10791/1773 500,000 1/15 D. D. & L. A.D.S.S./Forms/C. 2118.

Army Form C. 2118.

WAR DIARY
or
INTELLIGENCE SUMMARY.
(Erase heading not required.)

Instructions regarding War Diaries and Intelligence Summaries are contained in F. S. Regs., Part II. and the Staff Manual respectively. Title pages will be prepared in manuscript.

Place	Date	Hour	Summary of Events and Information	Remarks and references to Appendices
REGNAUVILLE	4.4.17	10 a.m.	18 O.R. arrived as reinforcement. ABR.	
MAILLY-MAILLET	5.4.17		Transport arrived from AMPLIER. ABR.	
	6.4.17.		Orders received from 174 Bde that 3 Coys. would be employed on Salvage work under I Corps Salvage Officer. 1 Coy under orders of R.T.O. COLINCAMPS. ABR.	
	7.4.17.		Salvage & Reihan work. Explosion at Salvage Dump, casualties — 3 O.R. killed, 1 Offr., 4 O.R. wounded.) 3 Coys. ABR.	
	8.4.17		Salvage & Reihan work continued. 2 BR.	
	9.4.17		Do. do. 2 BR.	
	10.4.17		Do. do. 2 BR.	
	11.4.17		2/Lt W.W. HUTTON joined as reinforcement.	
	12.4.17		Salvage & Reihan work. ABR.	
	13.4.17		do. do.	
	14.4.17		do. do.	
	15.4.17		Orders received from HQ 58th Division to march to rejoin 174th BRIGADE at BIHUCOURT. ABR.	
	16.4.17		Battalion marched to Camp near BIHUCOURT. (Ref. Map 57 C, G.N.W.) Route: AUCHONVILLERS — BEAUMONT HAMEL — MIRAUMONT — ACHIET LE PETIT — ACHIET LE GRAND — BIHUCOURT. ABR	

1577 Wt.W10791/1773 500,000 1/15 D. D. & L. A.D.S.S./Forms/C. 2118.

Army Form C. 2118.

WAR DIARY
or
INTELLIGENCE SUMMARY.
(Erase heading not required.)

Instructions regarding War Diaries and Intelligence Summaries are contained in F. S. Regs., Part II. and the Staff Manual respectively. Title pages will be prepared in manuscript.

Place	Date	Hour	Summary of Events and Information	Remarks and references to Appendices
BIHUCOURT	18.4.17		Battalion employed as working parties on roads	
	19.4.17		in neighbourhood of MORY - ECOUST Platoon Training	
	20.4.17			
	21.4.17		BRIG-GENERAL W. MACFRIGOR relinquished command of 174 INF. BDE. LT-COL. C.W. HIGGINS assumed " "	
			Battalion employed on road-work.	
	22.4.17		" "	
	23.4.17		" "	
	24.4.17		34 O.R. joined as reinforcements. Platoon & Company Training	

Charles W. Berkeley Lt. Col.
2/1st London Regt.

No 5

CONFIDENTIAL
****

WAR DIARY

OF

2/7th London Regt

From 25/4/17
To 24/5/17

WAR DIARY
or
INTELLIGENCE SUMMARY.

Army Form C. 2118.

Place	Date	Hour	Summary of Events and Information	Remarks and references to Appendices
BIHUCOURT.	25/4/17		Working parties. ADR	
	28/4/17		Working parties. ADR.	
	29/4/17 30/4/17		Two companies working, two carrying out Company Training. ADR	
	31/4/17		Working parties ADR	
	1/5/17		Two companies working, two training. ADR	
	2/5/17		Working parties. Two platoons A Coy at ECOUST, 1 killed, 5 wounded. ADR	
	3/5/17		Working parties. ADR	
	4/5/17		Company training. ADR	
	5/5/17		Company training. Afternoon 174 Bde. coys put through Gas Pluol. ADR	
	6/5/17		Battalion training. ADR	
	7/5/17		2/LT W.H. CUMMINGS + 2/LT S.B. SHANNON reported reinforcements. ADR	
	9/5/17		Battalion Training. ADR	
	10/5/17	5.30pm	Rehearsal of Brigade practice attack on LOUPART WOOD. Lieut. Col. C.D BERKELEY left for England. ADR	
	10/5/17		Brigade practice attack on LOUPART WOOD. ADR	
	12/5/17		Working parties. ADR	
	13/5/17		" Warning Order received that 174 Bde would relieve a Regt of El Divn in line at BULLECOURT. ADR	

Army Form C. 2118.

WAR DIARY
or
INTELLIGENCE SUMMARY.
(Erase heading not required.)

Instructions regarding War Diaries and Intelligence Summaries are contained in F.S. Regs., Part II. and the Staff Manual respectively. Title pages will be prepared in manuscript.

Place	Date	Hour	Summary of Events and Information	Remarks and references to Appendices
Bihucourt	14/5/17		All companies in Railway bank at ACHIET-LE-GRAND.	
	15/5/17		Battalion marched to camp near MORY (B.28.a.58), taking over camp of 2/1st LONDONS.	
	16/5/17			A/B
Mory	17/5/17		In camp near MORY finding working & carrying parties.	
	18/5/17		Orders received to relieve 2/8th London Regt. in support in Ecoust.	
		7.0 pm	Battalion (less Transport and Details) marched out to relieve 2/8th London Regt. Dispositions as under:-	
			HQ & B.D Coy. } Ecoust village	
			A Coy } Railway Embankment (U29.c.03 to U.29.d.24 approx)	
			C Coy } St LEGER Road near L'HOMME MORT (B.24.a.4)	
			on VAULX - IRAVOUR	
			Major E.N. FRENCH assumed the command of the Battalion.	
Ecoust	19/5/17	4.0 am	B.O.R. carried on as circumstances. Relief complete	
	20/5/17		Working & carrying parties furnished	
		8.15 pm	Orders received for 2 coys (A.B.) to relieve 2/6th LONDONS in S.E. crater of BULLECOURT	
			1 coy (less Lewis guns - B Coy) to join A Coy in Railway Embankment.	
	21/5/17	3.0 am	Battalion started to relieve 2/6th Londons allowed an attack against Bovis Trench - Bullecourt	
		10.0 am	2 Companies moved up to K. support 7/8 Londons in BULLECOURT	
			Orders received to relieve 2/6 LONDONS in BULLECOURT at night	
		9.30 pm	Relief commenced. Delayed through hostile barrage put down on Bullecourt vespasiana	
	22/5/17	2.30 am		
		11.30 pm	Relief complete. Dispositions as under for Trap (Appendix A)	
		5.0 am	Patrols sent out to Bovis Trench. (Appendix B)	

WAR DIARY
or
INTELLIGENCE SUMMARY.
(Erase heading not required.)

Army Form C. 2118.

Place	Date	Hour	Summary of Events and Information	Remarks and references to Appendices
BULLECOURT	22/5/17	7.30pm	Bombing posts under Cpl. Lydiard attacked Bovis Trench, working from U.14.a.03 westwards. Party driven back, & counter attack launched by enemy. Strength 150-200. Message sent back from A Coy to Battn H.Q. "Enemy attacking. Reinforcements." B. Coy moved up to reinforce. Enemy attack driven off by A Coy. Second enemy attack launched.	C.
		9-0pm	A Coy repulsed enemy with L.G. & rifle fire. See Appendix C.	Apt
		11-0pm	All quiet.	
	23/5/17		Relief commenced by 2/19. London Regt.	Apt
		5.30am	Relief complete. Battalion marched back to hut near Mory. (B 24 a.05)	
MORY	24/5/17		In camp at Mory. Working parties found for Bullecourt Avenue LE.	Apt
			Total casualties during tour 18/5/17 - 23/5/17 :-	
			Officers O.R.	
			Killed 1 12	
			Wounded 4 67	
			Missing - 5	APJ

Major
2/17th Batt
London Regt.

CONFIDENTIAL

WAR DIARY
of
2/4th LONDON REGT

from 4/5/15 to 4/9/15

WAR DIARY
or
INTELLIGENCE SUMMARY.

(Erase heading not required.)

Army Form C. 2118.

Instructions regarding War Diaries and Intelligence Summaries are contained in F. S. Regs., Part II. and the Staff Manual respectively. Title pages will be prepared in manuscript.

Place	Date	Hour	Summary of Events and Information	Remarks and references to Appendices

1577 Wt.W10791/1773 500,000 1/15 D.D.&L. A.D.S.S/Forms/C. 2118.

Army Form C. 2118.

WAR DIARY
or
INTELLIGENCE SUMMARY.
(Erase heading not required.)

Instructions regarding War Diaries and Intelligence Summaries are contained in F. S. Regs., Part II. and the Staff Manual respectively. Title pages will be prepared in manuscript.

Place	Date	Hour	Summary of Events and Information	Remarks and references to Appendices
MORY	25/5/17		In camp at MORY. Working parties found in BULLECOURT etc.	
	26/6/17			
	27/5/17			AB7
	28/5/17		Battalion relieved 2/1st LONDON Regt. in ECOUST. AAA	
ECOUST	29/5/17		Battalion relieved 2/10th LONDON Regt. in BULLECOURT. AAA	
BULLECOURT	30/5/17		Battalion in BULLECOURT. AAA	
	31/5/17		relieved in BULLECOURT by 2/10th LONDON Regt, & moved back to ECOUST. AB7	
	1/6/17		Battalion relieved in ECOUST by 2/10th LONDON Regt & moved back to camp at MORY. AAA	
	2/6/17		Battalion arrived in camp at MORY. Training + working parties - Casualties during tour 28/5/17 - 2/6/17 Killed 5 O.R. Wounded 32 -- (4 on at duty) AB7	
	3/6/17			
IN LINE	9/6/17		Battalion relieved 2/18th LONDON Regt. in Right Sub sector of Left sector (N.W. of BULLECOURT), under orders of 173rd INF. BDE. AB7	
	10/6/17		Holding line N.W. of BULLECOURT under orders of 173rd BDE. AB7	
	11/6/17			
	12/6/17		Battalion relieved in line by 2/1st LONDONS, marched back to camp at MORY (B27d) & reverted to orders of 174th Bde. Casualties during tour (other ranks killed 1, wounded 3. AB7	
	13/6/17			
Camp near MORY	14/6/17		Battalion moved to camp at B.21.c taking over from 2/5 BORDER Regt. AB7	
	15/6/17		B 15 c. 2/3 LONDON Regt. AB7	

Army Form C. 2118.

WAR DIARY
or
INTELLIGENCE SUMMARY.
(Erase heading not required.)

Place	Date	Hour	Summary of Events and Information	Remarks and references to Appendices
Mercatel	10/6/17		Battalion marched to relieve 2/5th Londons as Brigade Reserve Battalion in St. Leger. P.M.	
St Leger	14/6/17		In Brigade Reserve. P.M.	
	19/6/17		Battalion relieved 2/5th London Regt in Sector V14 c 29 to V 20 b 42. P.M. (Front Batt. left Sub-sector N.W. of Bullecourt).	
In the line	20/6/17 2/6/17 24/6/17		Holding line. P.M.	
	22-23 /6/17		Batt relieved by 1st S. Staffs Regt and marched back to St Leger. P.M. Casualties during Tour: Killed 1 Off, 6 O.R. Wounded 1 Off, 13 O.R.	
St Leger	23/6/17		Batt relieved by 2nd Queens and marched to Courcelles-le-Comte. A 15 d. etc. P.M.	
Courcelles	24/6/17 25/6/17 26/6/17 27/6/17 28/6/17 29/6/17 30/6/17		Training and Working Parties	

Noel French Lt Col.

WAR DIARY
of
2/5th London Regt.
1/4/17 to 31/7/17

Vol 7

Army Form C. 2118.

WAR DIARY
or
INTELLIGENCE SUMMARY.
(Erase heading not required.)

Instructions regarding War Diaries and Intelligence Summaries are contained in F. S. Regs., Part II. and the Staff Manual respectively. Title pages will be prepared in manuscript.

Place	Date	Hour	Summary of Events and Information	Remarks and references to Appendices
COURCELLES	1/4/17		Training and Working parties. ADD.	Ref Map 57C 1/40000
	2/4/17			
	3/4/17			
	4/4/17		Training and Working parties.	
	5/4/17		Battalion moved to Beaumetz. ADD.	
BANCOURT	6/4/17		BANCOURT (14.3.b.d.49). Route - SAPIGNIES - BAPAUME - BANCOURT. ADD.	
EQUANCOURT	7/4/17		Battalion moved to Beaumetz. EQUANCOURT (U.16.B.B.6). Route - BARASTRE - BUS - ETRICOURT - EQUANCOURT. ADD.	
	8/4/17		Battalion relieved 2/5th LEICESTERS and 2/5th LINCOLNS in the line Q.5.a.50 - Q.6.d.10. ADD	
	9/4/17		Relief complete 1.55 a.m. 10/4/17. ADD.	
In the line	10/4/17	3 a.m.	Enemy attempted a raid on A Company front, but was repulsed. Suffering enemy killed; A Coy casualties 1 O.R. killed, 6 wounded. ADD.	
	11/4/17		" ADD.	
	12/4/17		" ADD.	
	13/4/17		Patrol of 26 O.R. under 2/Lt GREGORY W.E. sent out to occupy BOAR COPSE mentioned at enemy party at N.E. corner of COPSE. Patrol withdrew; 1 O.R. wounded & missing. Patrol sent out again at nightfall & established in COPSE. ADD.	
	14/4/17		"	
	15/4/17		A+B Companies Alluding line from Q.5.d.8 to Q.6.d.u.) relieved by two Coys of 2/15 LONDON Regt & moved to positions in reserve to Left Left of Battalion front. ADD.	
	16/4/17		Battalion relieved in line by 2/15th LONDONS. Relief complete 8.0 p.m. Battalion withdrawn to Brigade Reserve in METZ EN-COUTURE. ADD.	
	18/4/17		Cleaning and inspections. ADD.	
	19/4/17		Working parties in line at night. Train of Spendu? ADD.	
	20/4/17			

Army Form C. 2118

WAR DIARY
or
INTELLIGENCE SUMMARY.
(Erase heading not required.)

Instructions regarding War Diaries and Intelligence Summaries are contained in F. S. Regs., Part II. and the Staff Manual respectively. Title pages will be prepared in manuscript.

Place	Date	Hour	Summary of Events and Information	Remarks and references to Appendices
METZ-EN-COUTURE	26/7/19		Working parties and Specialist Training continued. ABA.	
"	27/7/19		Working parties and Specialist Training continued. ABA.	
"	28/7/19		Battalion relieved by 3rd Battalion South African Infantry, & marched to BERTINCOURT area.	
BERTINCOURT	29/7/19		Battalion travelled by motor lorries to BAPAUME. Entrained at BAPAUME for new area. Detrained at BEAUMETZ-LES-LOGES and SAULTY. March to SIMENCOURT area.	
	30/7/19	1-30 am	Battalion in billets at SIMENCOURT. Platoons up & hat inspection. ABA.	
	31/7/19		Inspection of C+D Coys, A+B Coys bathed. Specialist classes. ABA.	

Noel French Lt Col

1577 Wt. W10791/1773 500,000 1/15 D. D. & L. A.D.S.S./Forms/C. 2118.

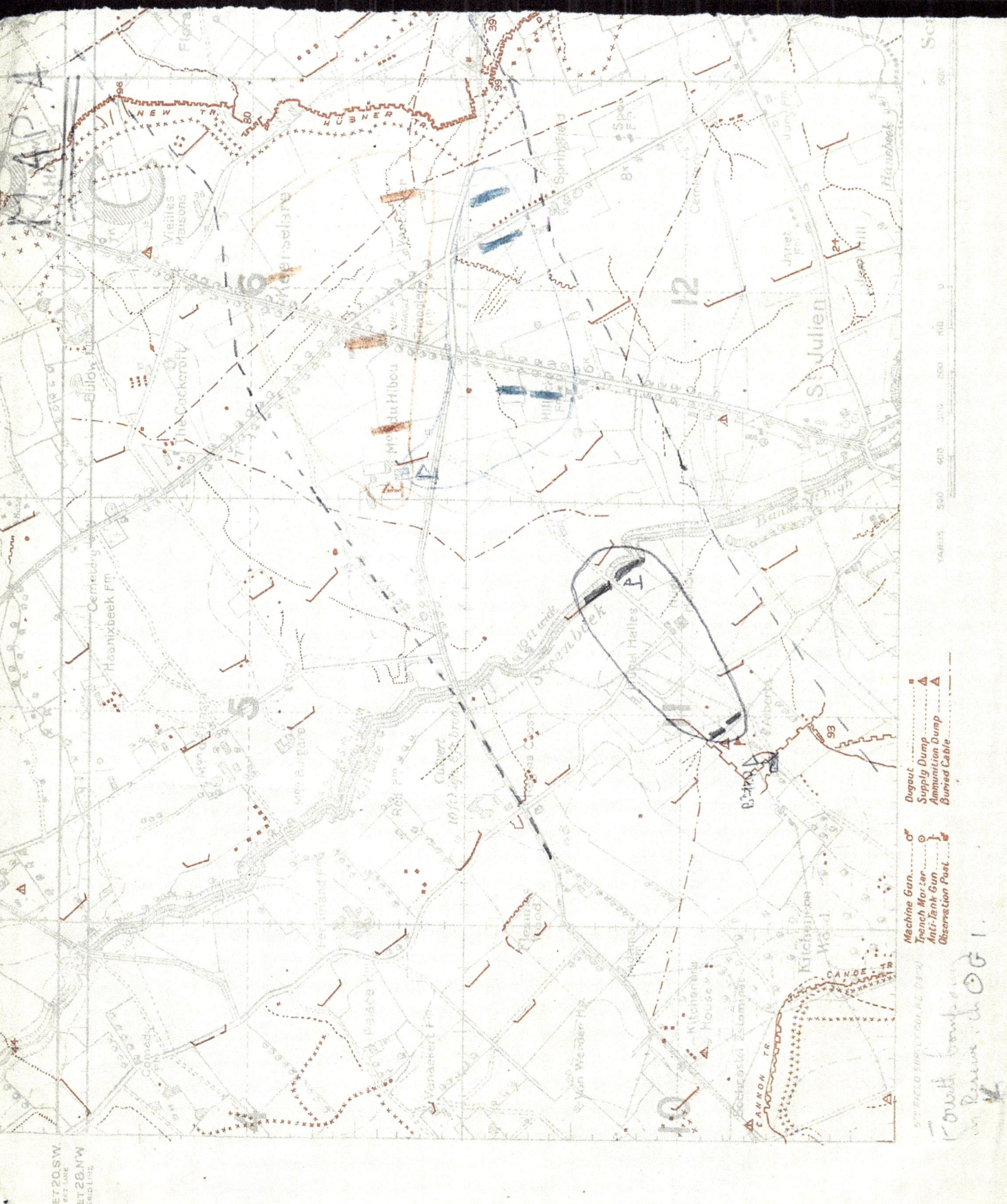

WAR DIARY or INTELLIGENCE SUMMARY

Army Form C. 2118.

2/4th London Regt.

Place	Date	Hour	Summary of Events and Information	Remarks and references to Appendices
SIMENCOURT	1/8/17		Baths & inspections.	
	2/8/17		Following officers joined as reinforcements: 2/Lt. C. EGRIE; 2/Lt. H.C. WOOLNER. 289.	
	3/8/17		Platoon Training. 289.	
	4/8/17		Platoon Parade. 289.	
	5/8/17		Platoon Training. 289.	
	6/8/17		Company Training. 289.	
	7/8/17		2/Lts. V.W. MILEHAM & 2/Lt. S. SCAMMELL joined for duty. 289. Brigade Route March. 2/Lt. H.C. STOCKEN joined for duty. 289.	
	8/8/17		Company Training. 289.	
	9/8/17		Battalion (less certain specialists) marched to BUTTE DE TIR, ARRAS. 2/Lt R.E. REA joined for duty, also 20 other ranks. 289.	
	10/8/17		Company Training. 289.	
	11/8/17		Church parade. Iron harm bus from left on A.A. Aircraft duties on dumps from 1/4th LONDONS. 289.	
	12/8/17		Company Training. 289.	
	13/8/17		Battalion Training & Brigade Training Area (near WAILLY). 289.	
	14/8/17		Battalion Training. Cut Out Scheme on ground N. of SIMENCOURT. 2/Lt. H.F.S. WILSON joined for duty. 289.	
	15/8/17		Brigade to Field exercise. 289.	
	16/8/17		Battalion Training & various fatigues at night. Dummy attack near BERNEVILLE. 20 other ranks joined for duty. 289.	

WAR DIARY
or
INTELLIGENCE SUMMARY.

(Erase heading not required.)

Army Form C. 2118.

Place	Date	Hour	Summary of Events and Information	Remarks and references to Appendices
SITTENCOORT	18/8/17		Kit inspection & Cttees. ABT.	
	19/8/17		Church parade. ABT.	
	20/8/17		General Fatigue Parades. ABT.	
	21/8/17		Ground Tactical Exercise. ABT.	
	22/8/17		Battalion training in Sunny areas. ABT.	
			54 other ranks joined from Base. ABT.	
	23/8/17		Bayonet parade for Lieut + large group. ABT.	
			74 other ranks joined from Base.	
			Battalion marched to ARRAs station, entrained. ABT.	
	24/8/17	1.15pm	Train left ARRAs.	
		5.54pm	Train arrived at GODEWAERSVELDE. Battalion detrained & marched to BROWN CAMP	
	25/8/17	1.30am	(A 22 + 86, SLW BELGIUM 28 NW (room) ABT.	
			Arrival at BROWN CAMP.	
		6.50am	Church parade. Commanding Officer & 11 other officers proceed to reconnoître line to be	
	26/8/17		taken over. ABT.	

Army Form C. 2118.

WAR DIARY
or
INTELLIGENCE SUMMARY.

(Erase heading not required.)

Instructions regarding War Diaries and Intelligence Summaries are contained in F. S. Regs., Part II. and the Staff Manual respectively. Title pages will be prepared in manuscript.

Place	Date	Hour	Summary of Events and Information	Remarks and references to Appendices
BROWYE CAMP POPERINGHE	27/8/17	2.30pm	Battalion marched from BROWNCAMP to relieve in CANAL BANK (C 25d) Rents- A30 central – VLAMERTINGHE – REIGERS BURG. Batt. nucleus (8 officers 135 O.R.) proceeded to Divisional Depot Battalion HOUTKERQUE.	Ref. Map Belgian 28 NW. Poperinghe ADS
CANAL BANK	28/8/17	2.0pm	Battalion moved by BATH ROAD to relieve 1/4th OXFORD - BUCKS and 1st BUCKINGHAM Battn. in line. A + B Coys in Front Line, C Coy in Support. D Coy in Reserve. Batt. H.Q. at ALBERTA (C 11 c 96). So Map A attd. Relief complete ADS	MAP A.
	29/8/17	2.30am	C & D Coys relieved A + B respectively. ADS	
	30/8/17		Inter Company relief complete ADS	
	31/8/17	1.0am		

Noel French, Lt.Col.

969

174/58

Confidential

WAR DIARY
of
2/4th Batt. The LONDON Regt
From 1/9/17 to 30/9/17

WAR DIARY
or
INTELLIGENCE SUMMARY.

(Erase heading not required.)

Army Form C. 2118.

Instructions regarding War Diaries and Intelligence Summaries are contained in F.S. Regs., Part II. and the Staff Manual respectively. Title pages will be prepared in manuscript.

Place	Date	Hour	Summary of Events and Information	Remarks and references to Appendices

1577 Wt.W10791/1773 500,000 1/15 D.D.& L. A.D.S.S./Forms/C. 2118.

Army Form C. 2118.

WAR DIARY
or
INTELLIGENCE SUMMARY.
(Erase heading not required.)

Instructions regarding War Diaries and Intelligence Summaries are contained in F. S. Regs., Part II. and the Staff Manual respectively. Title pages will be prepared in manuscript.

Place	Date	Hour	Summary of Events and Information	Remarks and references to Appendices
In the line	1/9/17		Holding the line. ABT	Map BELGIUM 28 NW 1/20000
	2/9/17		Battalion relieved in the line by 2/4th LONDONS. Two platoons B Coy remained in reserve. Relief complete 1-22 am. Battalion marched to billets in CANAL BANK, as Support Battalion of Brigade. ABT	
CANAL BANK	3/9/17		Cleaning & Inspection. ABT	
	4/9/17		Working parties and Baths. ABT	
	5/9/17		Working parties	
			Battalion relieved on CANAL BANK and marched to REIGERSBERG CAMP (about H.6.a.3.9.) ABT	
REIGERSBERG CAMP.	6/9/17		Training and Working parties. ABT Lt-Col E.W. FRENCH evacuated sick.	
	7/9/17		Training and Working parties. ABT	
	8/9/17		,, ,, ,, ,, ABT	
	9/9/17		Battalion marched to DAMBRE CAMP (B27 d 58.), taking over accommodation of 1/15 LONDON Regt. ABT	
D.AMBRE CAMP	10/9/17		Training. ABT	
	12/9/17		,,	
	13/9/17		26 O.R. rejoined from Butts Surplus. ABT	
	14/9/17		Training. ABT	
	15/9/17		Brigade tactical exercise. Enemy aeroplanes dropped bombs in vicinity of Battalion; casualties 9 O.R. wounded. ABT	
	16/9/17		Battalion moved to REIGERSBERG CAMP. (H6 a 39) ABT	
	17/9/17			

WAR DIARY or INTELLIGENCE SUMMARY

Army Form C. 2118.

Place	Date	Hour	Summary of Events and Information	Remarks and references to Appendices
REIGERS- BURG CAMP	18/9/17		Battalion relieved 2/2nd Battn. The London Regt. (R.F.) in line. JBA.	
IN LINE	19/9/17		Relief complete 2.45 a.m. JBA.	
	20/9/17		Battalion participated in 174 Inf. Bde's attack on German front line system. See Appendix 1A & our Maps attached JBA	
	21/9/17			
	22/9/17		Battalion relieved by 2/11th Battn. The London Regt. Relief complete 3-5 a.m. Battalion moved by tram to Camp at REIGERSBURG. JBA.	
REIGERSBERG			MAJOR S.L. HOSKING appointed to command Battalion.	
	23/9/17		Battalion marched to BRAKE CAMP. (H.30.d) JBA.	
BRAKE CAMP	24/9/17		Rest & refitting	
	25/9/17		Nucleus rejoined from HOUTKERQUE. JBA.	
	26/9/17			
	27/9/17		Battalion marched to entrain at BRIELEN; detrained at AUDRUICQ. Travelled from AUDRUICQ to billets in BONNINGUES, approx. 11-0 p.m. JBA.	
	28/9/17 29/9/17 30/9/17		Inspections & Training. JBA. Church Parade JBA.	

Mackenzie Lt Colonel Commanding 2/14th London Regt
Comg 2/14/17 2/14th London Regt.

Message Form.

..............................Division.

Map reference or mark own position on Map at back.

1. I am at..

2. I am at.. and am consolidating.

3. I am at.. and have consolidated.

4. Am held up at................................ by M.G. at................................

5. I need:—Ammunition.
   Bombs.
   Rifle Grenades.
   Water.
   Very lights.
   Stokes shells.

6. Enemy forming up for counter-attack at................................

7. Enemy withdrawing at..

8. I am in touch with................................ on Right / Left at................................

9. I am not in touch on Right. / Left.

10. I estimate my present strength at................................rifles.

11. Hostile {Battery / Machine Gun / Trench Mortar} active at................................

Time........................a.m. (p.m.)   Name................................

Date................................   Platoon............ Company............

    Battalion................................

Message Form.

..................Division.

Map reference or mark own position on Map at back.

1. I am at..

2. I am at.................................and am consolidating.

3. I am at.................................and have consolidated.

4. Am held up at........................by M.G. at...........................

5. I need:—Ammunition.
    Bombs.
    Rifle Grenades.
    Water.
    Very lights.
    Stokes shells.

6. Enemy forming up for counter-attack at.................................

7. Enemy withdrawing at.................................

8. I am in touch with.........................on Right/Left at...........................

9. I am not in touch on Right./Left.

10. I estimate my present strength at.................................rifles.

11. Hostile {Battery / Machine Gun / Trench Mortar} active at.................................

Time..................a.m. (p.m.)   Name.................................

Date.................................   Platoon................ Company................

                                    Battalion.................................

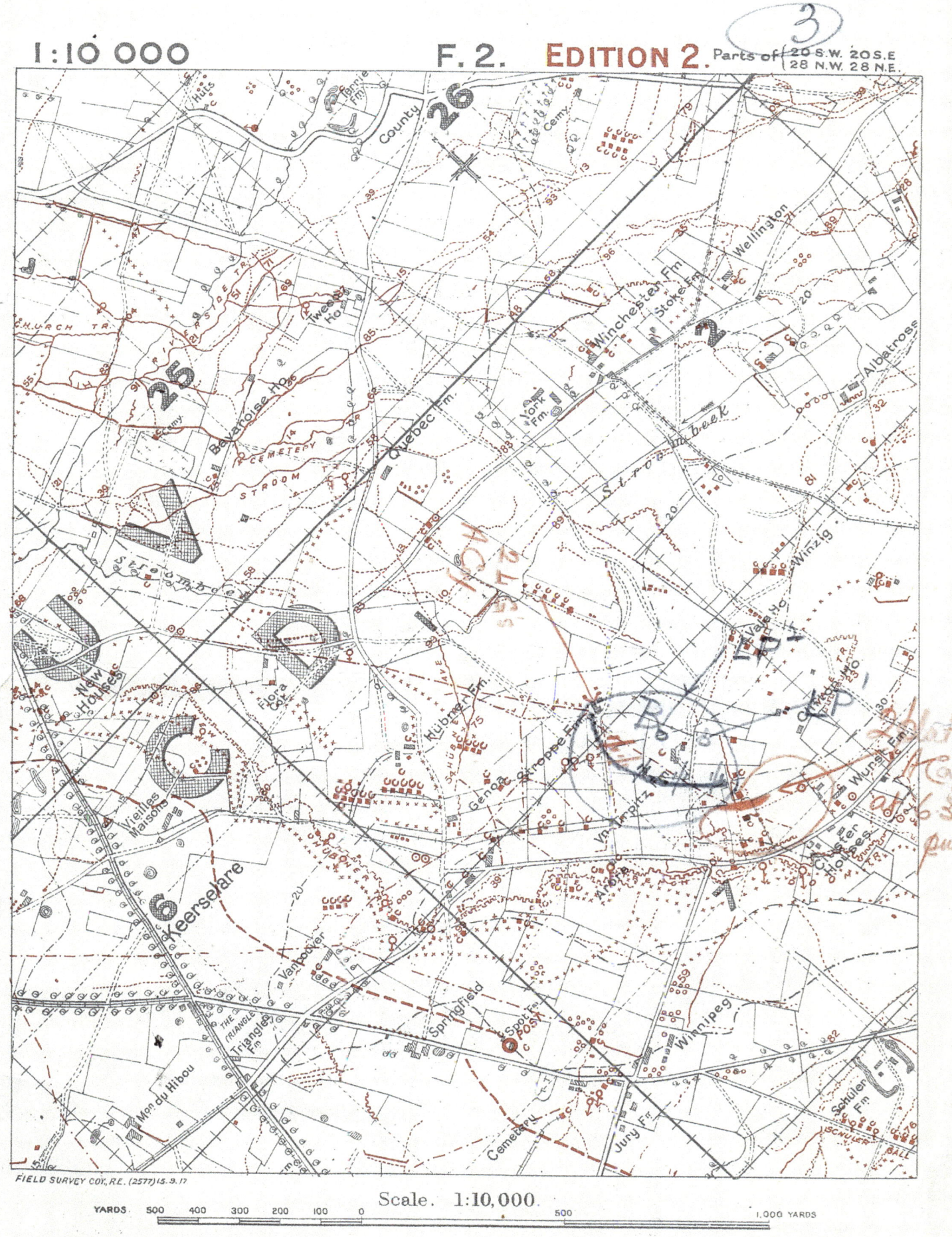

Message Form.

..........................Division.

Map reference or mark own position on Map at back.

1. I am at..

2. I am at....................................and am consolidating.

3. I am at....................................and have consolidated.

4. Am held up at..........................by M.G. at..........................

5. I need :—Ammunition.
   Bombs.
   Rifle Grenades.
   Water.
   Very lights.
   Stokes shells.

6. Enemy forming up for counter-attack at..........................

7. Enemy withdrawing at..........................

8. I am in touch with....................on Right / Left at..........................

9. I am not in touch on Right. / Left.

10. I estimate my present strength at..........................rifles.

11. Hostile { Battery / Machine Gun / Trench Mortar } active at..........................

Time.................... a.m. (p.m.)   Name..........................

Date..........................   Platoon.............. Company..............

Battalion..........................

Message Form.

............................Division.

Map reference or mark own position on Map at back.

1. I am at..

2. I am at.................................... and am consolidating.

3. I am at.................................... and have consolidated.

4. Am held up at .... by M.G. at..........................

5. I need :—Ammunition.
   Bombs.
   Rifle Grenades.
   Water.
   Very lights.
   Stokes shells.

6. Enemy forming up for counter-attack at ....

7. Enemy withdrawing at..

8. I am in touch with.............. at ....on Right / Left at..........................

9. I am not in touch on Right. / Left.

10. I estimate my present strength at.. rifles.

11. Hostile { Battery / Machine Gun / Trench Mortar } active at..

Time........................a.m. (p.m.)   Name..

Date..   Platoon.............. Company..............

Battalion..

2/7th. BATTALION, THE LONDON REGIMENT.

Report on period 18-22 September 1917.
Reference Map) POELCAPELLE edn. 3.1/10000 and maps annexed.

Day.	Time	Action	Reference Message or Orders.
-	-	-	
18	7 p.m.	Marched out of REIGERSBURG CAMP to relieve 2/2nd. London Regt.	
19	2.45 a.m.	Relief complete. Dispositions:-3) Platoons C Coy. in 6 forward posts, 1 Platoon in support. D Coy. 2 Platoons HIBOU 2) Platoons STEENBEEK. A & B Coys. CALIFORNIA DRIVE. Bn. H.Q. ALBERTA.	Map 1.
"	7.15 p.m.	C. Coy. put out posts forward of front tape line to cover assembly-shown in black pencil-support, platoon moved up to strengthen platoon weakened by forward posts and 1) Platoon D Coy moved up in support. Result of movement shown in pink pencil.	Map 1
20		Assembly effected without any interference.	
	4 a.m.	Withdrawal of covering parties complete. C & D Coys. moved to CALIFORNIA DRIVE. Casualties in Trench Tour 4 O.R. killed, 11 Wounded.	
	5.40 a.m.	C.O. reported at Bde. H.Q.	
	7.40 a.m.	Verbal order from Brigadier General Commanding to move Bn. forward to a position between HUBNER TRENCH and KEERSELARE-SPRINGFIELD ROAD.	
	8.10 a.m.	Bn. moved.	
	9.10 "	Tail of Bn. passed BUND.	
	10.35 "	A Coy. ordered by O.C. 2/5th. Bn. to move forward 300 yards or so to get in front of 2/8th. Bn. (Map 2 A2)	Map 2
	10.45 "	B Coy. ordered by 2/5th. Bn. to move and take up defensive line in and about STROPPE and TIRPITZ FARM to reinforce 2/5th. Bn. (Posts subsequently pushed forward in front of TIRPITZ on pink dotted line.)	Map 2 B2 (pink)
	11.30 "	O.C. 2/5th. returned to H.Q. at HIBOU informed me he had moved 2 of my Coys. A. & B to relieve congestion between HUBNER TRENCH & SPRINGFIELD KEERSELARE ROAD as 2/8th. were also in that neighbourhood. Copy message to B Coy attached. A. Coy. had verbal orders. (This move was reported to Bde. by O.C. 2/5th. Bn).	No) P. D. B*

-2-

Day	Time	Action.	Ref. Ms Message or Order.
20	1.30 p.m.	Verbal message brought by Lt. Harrison Jones that General that no Coys. of the 7th. Bn. were to be in advance of D"FUER. TRENCH. Message to A Coy. to withdraw to its original position. (Now complete 3.10 p.m.)	
	1.45 "	B.Coy. reported consolidating at STROPP FARM & TIRPITZ FARM. Adjutant obtained permission from B.G.C.(Littlejohns to Bde.Major) for B.Coy. to remain in its position B2.	
	4.15 "	Information from Bde. that enemy was advancing in strength on line AU WINCHESTER FARMS.	
	4.20 "	D Coy ordered to be ready to move to position near North & South track from D1 central to STROPP FARM. A.Coy warned to be ready to move to B. BN H.Q. in support.	
	4.40 "	B Coy informed of these movements.	
	5.30 "	B Coy saw enemy advancing on TIR- PITZ and sent to A Coy for reinforcements. 2 Platoons of A Coy arrived about 6.30 p.m. Dispositions of B Coy. & 2 Platoons of A Coy. at this time	MAP 3

On cessation of our barrage to organise thorough mopping-up parties but 4 patrols were sent out and 2 listening posts established by B Coy. ahead of their forward positions on the blue dotted line marked L.P.1 & L.P.2 on Map 3. Patrols covering the Coy. front in advance of listening posts and established touch with 2/5th in direction of WINTER FARM. The following is a report from 2Lt.L.J.Walsh on the subject of this counter attack

"Report of action taken. On afternoon of 20th. after our barrage ceased enemy were observed massing on rise East of "TIRPITZ". Pigeon message sent off at 5.30 also runner. Barrage started at 5.44 (?) and was most successful. Enemy advanced in formation apparently of 8 fours (i.e. a company platoon in col. of route) up to 1200 yards. Eight of these formations were seen at one time and probably twice as many were advancing on front from TIRPITZ to EGYPT FARMS. Am of opinion that at least 2000 of the enemy were visible from here in total advance. M.G. & L.G. caught them at 1500 to 1200 and some excellent results were obtained. One of B Coy L.G. caught a party with first burst causing several to fall and the circle to scatter. At 650 rifle fire assisted and squads of collective fire being opened on certain avenues

| Day. | Time | Action | Ref.Mess-or order. |

of advance and snipers held off along
the line. This held advance up until
open formation was adopted, enemy losing
heavily whole time. Short rushes were
then made. Shell holes affording good
cover. scattered parties got as close
250 and few odd men to 150. No really
determined organised attack was formed
from here for about 20 mins. And then the
barrage started. The effect of this was
beyond description, can make no estimate
of enemy losses as dust precluded good
observation but he stampeded, scattered parties getting into shell holes. Sniping
and L.G. work was continued until dark
in direction of any noise or light as no
movement could be detected though lights
were sent up from several points about 400
yards (at Nearest) away from our front
line. From daybreak this morning harrassing tactics have been employed and general
sniping indulged in along our line. M.G.s
and L.G.s getting busy on parties. This has
had effect in keeping down enemy fire but
parties gathering on ridge, messages were
sent up by pigeon and runner at 8 a.m. and
at 10.40 artillery opened with excellent
effect. Major Evans M.C, R.F.A. who was up
and sent message for artillery gave great
help in ranging for our snipers. Am of
opinion that it is of utmost importance
to keep up this harrassing fire. Few enemy
snipers have been at work but seemed to
have been knocked out. One enemy M.G. has
been quietened at apparently (as below) has
been sweeping us and shall be glad if this
area could be well burned as soon as possible. Area round D15.5 (1/5000). Suggest
necessity of S.F.A.line with O.P.here as
enemy M.G.may do damage during relief unless
they are burned as soon as fire is opened.
(Sd) L.E. Walsh. 2/Lt."

20 5.45p.m.   Verbal orders from B.O.C. to remove
               remainder of A Coy. to WIEST FARM to
               reinforce 6th. London and to come under
               orders of that Bn. Message to Coy. accordingly
20/21 12   Message B.M.A.424 timed 7.35 received
   midnight   ordering one Coy. to report to 6th Bn.
               and one Coy. to act as immediate
               counterattack Coy. against WIEST FARM

Day.	Time	Action.	Ref. Message or Order.

AREA, to be kept intact and to have their dispositions pointed out to them by Lt. Smith of M.G.Coy. and ordering the remaining Coy. to report to 2/8th. Bn to be used as a reinforcement ~~at 2/8th Bn~~ at HUBNER FARM.
Also that 2 Coys. 2/11th. Bn. were moving up to replace these Coys.

21. 12.10 a.m. Message to C.Coy to report to 2/8th.
     12.15 "   Message to D.Coy to move to WURST FARM and report to Lt. Smith.
                2/6th. and 2/8th. informed.
     1.25 "   D.Coy. Moved reported to 2/Lt Smith and took up position. move complete by 3.30a.m.
     3.30 "   Positions of A. B. & D. Coys. shown in   Map 4
                Note:-
                   C.Coy. Reported to 2/8th. Bn. and were ordered
                   to remain in their then position (i.e. as
                   shown on Map 2) until guides arrived.
                   These guides did not arrive and at a later
                   hour about 7 a.m. the movement of C.Coy.
                   was cancelled by verbal order of B.G.C.
     5.20 "   Message (untimed) that a practice barrage would be put down from 5.20 to 5.50. A, B & D Coys. stood to during barrage.
     7 a.m.   C & D. Coys. 2/11th. Bn. arrived and took up positions occupied by A & B. Coys. 2/7th Bn. shown on Map 2.

                Coy. Commanders of these two coys. instructed to reconnoitre route to HUBNER FARM and fire positions in D1 d and adjacent positions of parties of this Bde. so as to deal with any attempt by the enemy to advance up the STROOMBEEK VALLEY.
     6.15 "   Enemy barrage of considerable intensity put down on HIBOU, SPRINGFIELD-KEERSELARE ROAD, DIMPLE TRENCH and on the line GENOA-HUBNER.

                No information was received <u>at the time</u> as to where the attack was developing but later it appeared that 2/Lt. Walsh had reported to Attillery Officer at GENOA that there were no enemy parties in sight on our front and stated that barrage was not required and some of our shells were short. The enemy Very lights were reported to be getting nearer on the right but off the Bde front. Rifle Grenades or Trench Mortars were noted.
     7.5 p.m.   C.Coy. 2/11th. Bn. were moved to ARBRE.
                D.Coy. 2/11th. Bn. moved to HUBNER.
                C.Coy. 2/7th. Bn. ordered to be prepared to move at once on receipt of a further order.
     7.20 "   Leading Platoons of 2/10th. Bn. commenced to pass HIBOU and were sent forward to line SPRINGFIELD-KEERSELARE ROAD by their C.O.

Day.	Time.	Action	Ref. Message or orders.
	7.25 p.m.	Reported to Bde. 2 Coys. 2/10th. moving up as well as 2 of 2/11th.	
	7.40 "	Barrage began to die down and ceased by 8 p.m.	
	8.0 "	2/Lt. Shillito sent out to find the 2 Coys. of 2/11th. and to put them on the way to carry out their relief. This Officer took instructions to A.B.&D Coys. as to withdrawal.	
22	3.5 a.m.	Relief reported complete. Companies returned to HIGUISBERG.	

Casualties from Zero hour to arrival in
HIGUISBERG on 22nd.
    1 Officer Capt. H.S.Green killed.
    1 Officer 2/Lt. E.R.Cummines wounded.
    O.R.   16 killed.
           76 wounded.
           5 missing.

F.Morking.
Lieut. Colonel
Commanding 2/7th. Battalion.
The London Regiment.

24.9.17.

APPENDIX I.

Report on action taken by B. Coy. 2/7th. Bn. London Regt.

Report as to development of Counter attack on afternoon of 20th. is included in Battalion report attached. The following particulars as to the action taken by this Company may be of interest.

The enemy was seen in Platoon in fours on the ridge behind BRUNHILDE FARM advancing West. Fire was opened by L.Gs. at 1800 yards. The first burst from one of these guns scattered a Platoon which reformed 50 yards nearer us and were again caught by the same gun and dispersed - they were never seen to reform again. At 1500 yards definite squads were organised for collective rifle fire and considerable execution was done on successive parties of the enemy following the same track as they passed the ranging points. The M.Gs. opened fire later and as a result the enemy had to stop for 20 minutes to reform in a hollow near ALBATROSS FARM. By this time additional ranges were announced to the men and when the enemy commenced to move again in extended lines, fire was opened by all rifles and Lewis Guns at a range of 1000 yards. At 750 yards the order was given for independent firing owing to the broken nature of the ground. From this range to 200 yards Officers Sergeant Major, Signallers and Runners joined in the shoot. The enemy tried to make use of the trench elements in D8 a. This enabled them to attempt a final attack formation at about 200 yards in front of our position. Three times this line was broken by M.G., L.G., and rifle fire, eventually a few men got as close as 75 yards when our barrage arrived and nothing more could be seen of the attack.

Heartened by this experience this company set about the enemy on the following morning at dawn. Two scouts per Platoon each taking a definite area, fired on all movement under orders from their fire leader. When the light improved 20 men were told off as snipers and an order was given to all section leaders to see that no enemy movement was possible.

About 9 a.m. on the 21st the Boche snipers and two M.G's began to worry us, one M.G. was located, two L.G's turned on to it and when the other Boche M.G. team attempted to move to a new position on our left flank, the team was laid out and the gun apparently disabled as it was abandoned. A message as to the location of the other Boche M.G. was sent to the Artillery with the result stated in Battn. report. The Boche snipers were disposed of by a three post system and by mid-day his sniping had ceased.

[signature]
Lieut. Colonel.
Commanding 2/7th. Battalion,
The London Regiment.

24.9.17.

APPENDIX II.

I have the honour to report on communications during the recent Battle as follows:-

O.L. Lamps were used to great advantage both by day and night and are undoubtably the best means of communicaticons over such country.

Louvre Shutters became of great value for inter-company and platoon communication.

Pigeons were also of value.

Message Rockets. These we found no necessity to use.

Semaphore, was used with considerable success for inter-company and platoon work and saved heavy and risky work on the Runners. I cannot too highly recommend this method of signalling forward of Battalion Headquarters and to my mind every man should possess a knowledge of it.

Phone communication forward of Battalion Headquarters was not possible

Power Buzzers were not very useful during heavy shelling owing to the constant breaking of base wires, but during comparative quiet periods they were certainly of value.

[signature]

Lt Colonel
Commanding 2/nth Battalion The London Regt

8. 174/5/2 Vol 10

CONFIDENTIAL

War Diary
7th Batt- The London Regt.
from 1/10/14 to 31/10/14

Army Form C. 2118.

WAR DIARY
or
INTELLIGENCE SUMMARY.
(Erase heading not required.)

Instructions regarding War Diaries and Intelligence Summaries are contained in F. S. Regs., Part II. and the Staff Manual respectively. Title pages will be prepared in manuscript.

Place	Date	Hour	Summary of Events and Information	Remarks and references to Appendices
BONNINGUES-LEZ-ARDRES	11/10/17 – 8/11/17		Platoon Training. AAA	Ref Map HAZEBROUCK 1/100,000 BELGIUM Sheet 23 NW 1/20,000
	9/11/17 – 13/11/17		Company Training. AAA	
	14/11/17 – 19/11/17		Battalion Training. AAA	
	20/11/17		Battalion marched to entrain at AUDRUICQ; detrained at HOPOUTRE, marched to billets in POPERINGHE. Portion of transport made the journey by march route via LEDERZEELE AAA.	
POPERINGHE	21/11/17 22/11/17 23/11/17		In POPERINGHE. AAA	
	24/11/17		Battalion marched to SIEGE CAMP (B2c). AAA	
SIEGE CAMP	25/11/17		Battalion (less transport) marched to CANAL BANK. AAA	
	26/11/17	8.30am	Battalion moved up from CANAL BANK	
		10.15am	Reached CANE TRENCH (C.9.c.) Bonn under orders of G.O.C. 173rd Brigade.	
		10.50am	Message received from 173rd Bde. to move up to ROSE TRENCH; H.Q. at V.19.a.7.	
		11.15am	Battalion shift to move from CANE TRENCH	
		10pm	Battn. H.Q. reached V.19.a.7. Battalion reported in position between PHEASANT FARM and ST-JULIEN–POELCAPELLE Road.	

Army Form C. 2118.

WAR DIARY
or
INTELLIGENCE SUMMARY.
(Erase heading not required.)

Instructions regarding War Diaries and Intelligence
Summaries are contained in F. S. Regs., Part II.
and the Staff Manual respectively. Title pages
will be prepared in manuscript.

Place	Date	Hour	Summary of Events and Information	Remarks and references to Appendices
In the line	26/10/17	4-30 pm	Battalion moved from position of Support to relieve 2/4 & 2/24 London Regts. in Right subsector of Brigade front. JRH	
		11-30 pm	Relief complete. Dispositions. D Coy at TRACAS FARM C – MEUNIER FARM A – BEEK HOUSES B – in support to C Coy H.Q at GLOUCESTER FARM	
	27/10/17	12 noon	Verbal orders from Bde. that Battn to relieve 2/1st LONDONS in left subsector with two support Coys. JRH	
		1-05 pm	Orders to A & B Coys as to relief and to C & D Coys as to redistribution in right subsector.	
		2-0 pm	Relief to Battn H.Q. moved from GLOUCESTER FARM. A & B Coys began to withdraw from support positions.	
		4-115 pm	Battn. H.Q. arrived V.19.a.9.7.	
		9-50 pm	Relief in Left subsector complete. JRH	
	28/10/17	8-0 a.m	Message + disposition map received from O.C. A Coy, shewing NOBLE'S FARM not occupied by us.	
		4-45 pm	Head of 2/16 LONDONS reached V.19.a.9.7.	
		8-25 a.m	Completion of relief of Battalion by 2/16 LONDONS. Battalion moved to MERRIS PARK. JRH

1577 Wt W10791/1773 500,000 1/15 D. D. & L. A.D.S.S./Forms/C. 2118.

Army Form C. 2118.

WAR DIARY
or
INTELLIGENCE SUMMARY.
(Erase heading not required.)

Instructions regarding War Diaries and Intelligence Summaries are contained in F. S. Regs., Part II. and the Staff Manual respectively. Title pages will be prepared in manuscript.

Place	Date	Hour	Summary of Events and Information	Remarks and references to Appendices
KEMMEL PARK	29/10/17	11.45 a.m.	Battalion moved to CANAL BANK, a Battalion in Brigade Reserve. AMS.	
CANAL BANK	30/10/17		Gn CANAL BANK.	
		2-0 pm	D. Coy moved up to PHEASANT TRENCH as Coy in support to Battalion in the Line. AMS	
	31/10/17	1.45 pm	Battalion 2 marched to SIEGE CAMP	
		8.45 pm	D. Coy rejoined Battalion at SIEGE CAMP. AMS	

Mackenzie
Lieut Colonel
Cmr? 2/17 Bn London Reg¹.

WAR DIARY or INTELLIGENCE SUMMARY.

(Erase heading not required.)

Instructions regarding War Diaries and Intelligence Summaries are contained in F. S. Regs., Part II. and the Staff Manual respectively. Title pages will be prepared in manuscript.

Place	Date	Hour	Summary of Events and Information	Remarks and references to Appendices
SIEGE CAMP	1/4/17		Rest and refit. Bttn.	
	2/4/17		-	
	3/4/17		Sun officers - 3.15 OR (Capt. W.D. COLERIDGE in command) moved to CANAL BANK to provide daily working party under orders of 58th Divl Signals R.E.	
	4/4/17		Training. Bttn.	
	5/4/17		Battalion (less Transport and Details) moved to E. CANAL BANK, where working party rejoined. Bttn.	
	6/4/17		Company officers reconnoitred line Bttn.	
CANAL BANK	7/4/17		Battalion relieved 2/10 LONDONS in POELCAPELLE sector. Defences.	
	8/4/17		Battalion relieved Left Bn: A Coy Centre: C - Right: D - Support: B - Bttn HQ at V.19.b.71	
	9/4/17		Battalion was relieved in line by 2/6th LONDONS. Relief complete 7.50 p.m. Marched to KEMPTON PARK, thence by lorry to SIEGE CAMP.	

Army Form C. 2118.

WAR DIARY
or
INTELLIGENCE SUMMARY.
(Erase heading not required.)

Place	Date	Hour	Summary of Events and Information	Remarks and references to Appendices
SIEGE CAMP	1-16.4.17		Rest, refitting & training in SIEGE CAMP. AAA.	
HERZEELE	17/4/17		Battalion marched to ELVERDINGHE; thence by train to HERZEELE. Battle surplus & reinforcements joined from Divisional Depot. Battalion. AAA	
	18/4/17		Company Training. AAA.	
	19/4/17		Company & Specialist Training.	
	20/4/17		Advance parties proceed to new area. AAA.	
	21/4/17			
	22/4/17 to 24/4/17		Company & Specialist Training. AAA.	
	25/4/17		Battalion marched to camp near PROVEN. Transport starts by road for new area. AAA.	
	26/4/17		Battalion entrained at PROVEN; detrained at WIZERNES; marched to billets at BAYENGHEM. Fly chairs in Transport joined Battalion at BAYENGHEM. AAA.	bivouacs
	27/4/17		Battalion and Transport marched to billets at SELLES. AAA.	
	28/4/17 29/4/17 30/4/17		Platoon Training. AAA.	

Army Form C. 2118.

2/7 London Regt

WAR DIARY
or
INTELLIGENCE SUMMARY.
(Erase heading not required.)

Instructions regarding War Diaries and Intelligence Summaries are contained in F. S. Regs., Part II. and the Staff Manual respectively. Title pages will be prepared in manuscript.

Place	Date	Hour	Summary of Events and Information	Remarks and references to Appendices
SELLES	1.12.17		Platoon Training. Bn.	
	2.12.17		Platoon Training. Bn.	
	3.12.17			
	4.12.17		Musketry Party firing at BLEQUIN. Range of Lewis & Rifle Meets. Bn.	
	5.12.17		Platoon Training Bn.	
	6.12.17		Musketry Party & Platoon Training Bn.	
	7.12.17		Battalion moved by march route from SELLES to JENNINGHEN Bn.	
SENINGHEM	8.12.17		Battalion moved from JENNINGHEN to WIZERNES Entrained at ELVERDINGHE & marched to DIRTY BUCKET CAMP. Bn.	
ELVERDINGHE	9.12.17		Battalion marched from DIRTY BUCKET CAMP to KEMPTON PARK C.15.b.4. Bn.	
KEMPTON PARK	10.12.17		Wiring & 200 OR. attached to 255 Tunnelling Coy. C26.b.3. Working Parties Bn.	July 26
	11.12.17		Working Parties. Bn.	
	12.12.17			
	...			
	20.12.17		Working Parties Bn.	
	26.12.17		Working Parties. 25 additional OR. attached to 255th Tunnelling Coy. Bn.	
	27.12.17			
	28.12.17		Working Parties Bn.	
	30.12.17			
	31.12.17		Working Parties. 25 additional OR attached to 255th Tunnelling Coy. Bn.	

J.H. Hoskins
Lt Col

WAR DIARY or INTELLIGENCE SUMMARY

Army Form C. 2118

2/7 London

Place	Date	Hour	Summary of Events and Information	Remarks and references to Appendices
KEMPTON PARK	1.1.18 – 4.1.18		Working Parties in forward areas. AAA	SHEET 1 22. 1/10,000
	5.1.18		Working Parties. 2 O.R. additional attached to 253 Tunnelling Coy R.E. AAA	
	6.1.18 7.1.18		Working Parties. AAA	
	8.1.18		Battalion (less 10 offr. 775 OR.) attd. 253 Tunnelling Coy & other small attachments) marched from KEMPTON PARK to entrain at BOESINGHE. Detrained at PROVEN; marched to Camp at ROAD CAMP (F254)	SHEET 17 1/40,000
			Transport proceeded by road. AAA	
			Blown in Officers. Photographs required. AAA	
			Kit inspection. AAA	
ROAD CAMP	9.1.18 10.1.18		Training. AAA	
	11.1.18 12.1.18		G.O.C. & Coys paraded and written to recruits of 17th Bn. AAA	
			Lt-Col. G.L. HOSKING left Bn. & E.J.McLean. Lt. E.H. IRELAND assumed Bn². under comt. AAA	
	13.1.18		Training. AAA	
	14.1.18 15.1.18		Training. AAA Advance party under ⁄Lt. R.E. STEVENSON left for new area. AAA	
	16.1.18 17.1.18 18.1.18		Training. AAA	
	19.1.18		Battalion left ROADCAMP 9.30pm & marched to entrain at PROVEN. AAA	OO 2.

Army Form C. 2118.

WAR DIARY
or
INTELLIGENCE SUMMARY.
(Erase heading not required.)

Place	Date	Hour	Summary of Events and Information	Remarks and references to Appendices
PROVEN	20.1.18	11:30am	Train. Capt. PROVEN.	Ref. Map ATH 1/100,000
		3-4pm	Battalion detrained at VILLERS-BRETONNEUX; marched to billets in MOREUIL + MORISEL. ASP	
MOREUIL	21.1.18		Company Training. ASP	
	25.1.18			
	26.1.18		Brigade Route March. ASP	
			Company Training. ASP	
	28.1.18		G.C.M on LT E.H. IRELAND. Verdict: Not Guilty. ASP	2/Lt. 6 B.E.
	29.1.18		Company Training	
	30.1.18		Battalion moved by march route to billets in DOMART-SUR-LA-LUCE. 2/LT. 93 O.R. (preceded by Adv. party 1 Bn MIDDLESEX B/7074.) ASP	
			LT E.H. IRELAND, 2/LT. W/S. WILSON 2/LT. R. KNOX.	
	31.1.18		Ref. (Authority:- AG/B/74 (O) and G.HQ. 3rd Echelon B/7074.	
			Company Training	

Commanding 2/7th R. Sussex Rgt.

www.ingramcontent.com/pod-product-compliance
Lightning Source LLC
Chambersburg PA
CBHW081452160426
43193CB00013B/2452